ABOUT THE AUTHOR

Emily Rose was the first female Staffordshire Poet Laureate (2017-2019) before becoming Poet in Residence at Lichfield Library and co-host of Spoken Word night WordCraft in Stoke-on-Trent. Performing regularly across the UK, Emily has a repertoire of poetry that tackles mental health, emotional wellbeing and the complications of human relationships, and was most recently placed in the Top 5 Shortlist for Culture Recordings' New Voice in Poetry Prize 2020.

Twitter: @EmilyRose_Poet
Instagram: by.emily.rose

Emily Rose Galvin
the dew point

VERVE
POETRY PRESS
BIRMINGHAM

PUBLISHED BY VERVE POETRY PRESS
https://vervepoetrypress.com
mail@vervepoetrypress.com

FIRST PUBLISHED SEP 2021

Printed and bound in the UK
by ImprintDigital, Exeter

ISBN: 978-1-912565-63-4

Cover image by the author.

here's to the mess we make

CONTENTS

Acknowledgements

the dew point

Bossiney

You're standing at the handrail overlap
of the shore,
as I linger over fading rockpool scars.
Snapping crab and limpet flint mimic
the splinter of your safety under curious fingernails,
while cat tongue sea - it laps
ankle deep
at the danger space between us:

wadeable
but uncomfortable.

neap tide
the lifeguard had whispered
or maybe it was the rocks.
Maybe majesty moon herself, at three quarter bloat,
supping at the earth with indecision.
Mouth like iced wine, pebbledash taste buds,
ecstasy foamed across sand-anchored feet.

You looked away
so I'll take
      five   steps   further   to the tide
and let the sting of salt against my denim calves
decide
what is to be done with me.

(i)

sad is
the meat juice
leaking between ribs / squeezed by hearts too salt-fat /
arrhythmic / it's the wet creak of hearts when sun-dried
and tear-preserved / it's the smell of the soil after
tears and probing noses of worms / it's rolling every
memory around your teeth like tiny painful marbles /
it's spitting them into sinks and jars / it's
jars
and
jars
of heartache labelled mauve and plum / it's listening to the
way each mauve sings like a particular shade of rain / it's
too sunshine / too shaded treetop / it's every kind of tree
planted on an ocean bed / it's knowing none of the jars
have the right tint of sea / it's plunging the sink with
tempered fist to find the right tint of marble / it's finding
memory that paints like saline rain / it's so much
salt
in
jars
and
the aching kind of sound you get
when you place the right shell to your ear
and
hear
silence.

Borrowed

Tell me

is it theft
to lift your scent from the books I borrow?
To bathe behind closed eyelids in the spice of your
existence
and hold the pages close, as senses dance
with forearm stretch
nicotine carnation
leather dusk and firebug tongue.

For if our lives are destined to be separate;
if I can never freely sample the jawline nectar of your skin
then
make a villain of me.
I'll steal every ounce of you I can lay a fingertip on.

the dew point

I like to take baths with the window open.

The rise of steam is like watching floating fragments
of soul,
dense with salt and dirt and tiny pieces of melancholy.
Most of it gets caught on the glass pane,
metamorphosed, finds itself bloated and snail trailed,
threatening to blackhead the tiles below.
But some -
I see the ghosted billows of bathroom window runaways
eloping with the clouds.

In this light, I can't tell if they're gunmetal, or coral,
or nectarine,
but I do know they look weightless,
carrying all my weight.

I don't want to touch them.

And the glassy bead of sweat from your nose
dropped on to my chin
so we wrung the sheets and basked in our parched
lightness.

And I picked salt crystals from between my toes and
wondered where all the sea went from beneath them.
And do the clouds carry your pain too?

Are they amber now?

And I'm trying to drain the pools that cling to the railings
of your eyelids
but they keep filling
though I've tried every finger now.

None are the right temperature.
Not cloud-like at all.

Paradiso

Never a kiss like this -
feathered blankets on goose-pricked skin,
a summer sun's tongue on stomach
      shoulder.
      shin.
I took his warmth as if I'd lived forever frozen.
Swapped my black sky nightgown for cloudless skies,
      breeze whipped skirts
      idle Sundays.
I took him as rebirth,
tongue-mapped constellations,
as his lips
carved monuments;
those knee-buckle flutters
that black and white film reels would call love.

The Colour Picked Without Thought

Street Lamp Yellow, we called it;
the lemon curd coating
that pinpricks this 12am street;
the effervescence of light pulled down by
its concrete grounding.

My fingers feel like that, sometimes.
These spindles of marrow, adorned with streetlights,
so desperate to root themselves in harm.
So I look to the sky instead.
Cassiopeia, she winks at me,
with all the boastfulness I wish I could own.
She appears to me tonight upside down,
clinging to her steadfast indignity and I wonder how it
feels to be so
constant.

The late-night sparrow is a bubble of ocean,
and I remind myself that I am concrete
rooted to this earth.
and that I cannot connect to these unearthly thoughts
and that I feel more Andromeda than Cassiopeia;
bound to the tarmac stretching rocks.
Still,
I can't help but shed a tear for those throne-chained stars -
us all so bound by the rules of Street Lamp Yellow
and yet so almost-close to the sky.

Pink

The moon was pink

blushing, apple blossomed, heart-cell saturated, babygirl
wallpapered, coral and peaching, naked flush, fleshed and
open, cherry stoned, fairy cake sprinkling, yawning eyed,
strawberry finger stained, salmon stomach, puppy tongue,
rosebud mouth, lipstick teeth, shell glossed, sunset shadow
lonely.

The moon was pink, in different cities,
and the wind sounded like a sigh.

Slow Jazz

Slow jazz plays
so the subtitles say -
a single noted, heart laden singlet.
The musical metaphor for
a silent tear
a British cry.

And you know these tears don't spring
for fictional entities,
no matter their plight or humanity;
their scripted stories
or, horoscope like, the way each plot-line subtlety blends
somewhere in to your own first-world soap opera.

Slow jazz plays,
but you birth the loaded lamentation of each
disappointment, heartache and error.
That alcohol-slick spill, leaked with each individual
overturning
of the paper cup, aorta lined building blocks of your
unsteady soul.
Those that fizzled and tumbled with every heart opened.
Disintegrated with each unwitting fly trap sprung.
Stacked, then faltered with each realisation
that you didn't ask for it to be like this
but you're incapable of escaping.

Slow jazz plays
and the tribal drumbeat is building in the base of your
throat now.
Bass-lines built from regret and ambition:
to open your mouth would be to let out the perfect,
worldly harmonisation of solidarity and belonging,
of escaping and setting root,
of sorrow, and sorrow that sorrow got in the way of hope,
and you cry because you're sorry.

But you could never say it.

Not in the way that you mean it.

So, you'll probably send over a playlist.
Heartfelt,
misinterpreted,
one where slow jazz plays.

From the Farmer's Market, Just Outside

There's a woman eating oranges
in the library.
Sliding each segment from the shucks of a half open rucksack.
I saw her carrying them earlier in a plastic carrier bag
from the farmer's market, just outside.
And the smell is unmistakable,
wafting between the bookshelves with a tangible, tangerine tint.
I turn to you,
flagrantly collecting sweet wrappers as battlements
around coffee cup castles,
and almost say
who's got oranges?
before I see her eyes -
jittered, danger flitting.
Twitching, rabbit eyes, meekly camouflaged
by tangling headphones wires.
And I'm not quite sure what your secret is,
orange lady,
but I promise it will stay between us.

Gold

Arched back and frantic shoulders.
Grinding hands,
fabric against fabric,
ringing misted droplets of fire from dampened cotton.
And you watch in fear
as crimson flirts with bath water,
teasing out that final watermark of *shame*.

Shame
should the male gaze fall upon your embarrassment.
The stain of your essence.

Shame
should the ebb and flow of your body remind him
that Mother Nature's bloodied teeth lie
between your thighs
instead of his dominance.

Shame
that the warmth which brought the flush of sex
to your cheek
now brings a shielded scorn
a curling lip

A shame
that the power which runs through your veins
and through the veins of his mother
could be treated as poison.
That gilded strength,
that treasured femininity,
that falling fruit, ripened into blood orange
and goldenberry.

Tinnitus

Did you hear that noise?
It's not quite
a roar
but it's breaking waves and riptides full of bird whistles
ringing and racing down the corridors of your ears
and
            that's yours now.

Blink and the vision is just blind eyes wondering
why there are so many
people.
Their mouths are moving,
gaping fish counter
mouths,
glass eyeballs lolling like loose tongues.

Blink and it's all
Police reports and smashed up walls and it all sounds like
the same mouth/the same ears are ringing and I know
conversation is still spilling out in front of me like
a cut throat.

Blink and it's all
kicked ribs on the pavement and counting my own,
delicate as they are,
and wondering which one will be next.
Or which garnet-glass gawking eye
or hooked fish mouth
to cut my loosening tongue.

and I Still Can't Find My Passport

Then, we sat on readjusted second-hand furniture,
and stole microwave popcorn
from each other's plastic bowls.
And we talked
about bohemia,
about cities,
green fairies, and rooftops, and the side of the world
that the moon kissed this morning.

When I am with you there's no place I'd rather be -
I still don't understand that line
but I did,
then.

Watching black and white portraits
in a makeshift movie theatre -
the creased sheet idols foretold the asymmetry
of our dreams.

But we didn't know that,
then.
The folded faces were the pinnacle of
our sky-gazed fantasies.

The sheets need ironing, these days.
The popcorn maker -
I trace our fire engine initials in the dust across the lid.
When I am with you
you ask me
where I went.

I don't think I have an answer,
so I look for us in wrinkles straight out
of the washing machine,
in mottled cork edges,
in the tired eyes of Celia Johnson.

I put us somewhere safe.

I can't remember where I was.

Ryan Gosling's Curtains

That poem
he said
it's like Ryan Gosling's face at the end of La La
Land. You know the bit in the Jazz Club?

and I smiled and said I did.

I didn't say
> *I wrote about La La Land this time last year*

I didn't say
> *you've still got that little curl of hair, the one*
> *that whispers with your eyelashes when you*
> *concentrate*

I didn't say
> *we don't watch that film anymore*
or
> *does that film feel like looking in a mirror to*
> *you too?*
or
> *where are we going?*

I smiled and said I did.
We carried on driving,
and you didn't check your mirrors.
Not once.
We passed by a car crash.
We didn't slow down.

To Dad: For Mom

This morning
the lines around Mom's eyes seemed darker.
Wiser.
Deeper,
but not in the way that signals ticking of clocks,
falling of leaves -
more like sanded erosion.
The riverbeds of dried-up,
tear-track flash floods.

So I asked,
this morning,
if she was sleeping okay,
and interruption told me
that each night
Mom talks to you while you sleep,
without expectation of reply or acknowledgment.
Just talks.
From bedtime
until morning.
I suppose in an attempt to monitor your well-being,
and I suppose
to soak in every moment of your, albeit silent, presence.

This morning
I asked Mom if I could help,
though the words felt foolish
as they tripped past my teeth,
because I wanted to tell her to try writing.
In those lonely 1am, 4am, forever am hours,
I wanted to tell her to pour her troubles out
through spilling words,
and this morning
when I wanted to tell Mom to write,
I figured,
maybe I should write.

Write this morning.
About that morning.

About weighted panic.
About tidal fish tank ripples that suddenly make life
feel like swimming backwards.
About the creeping change slighting through our arteries,
vaguely morphing the shape of our appleseed core,
but I can't seem to let it out.
I can't let the words slip under the *I'm fine* barrier
that perches, owl-eyed, at the tip of my tongue.
And when someone asks
How are you doing?
there are now so many adjectives lodged in the throated
mucus of guilt.

Guilt that
I'm okay.

Okay because I'm yet to process.
Okay
because my mental cogs still haven't whirred through issues
like
the essence of life,
and no life,
and mortality, and love, and family, and what the fuck
is right and wrong
and this morning
I envy Mom.

Mom and her rivers of worry.

Mom and her endless nightlight talking

because
we're all scared,
but at least she has something to say.

Escargot

Have you ever watched a person eat escargot?
Delicate, but brutal.
Remember that the finest parts are most likely to hide
so initial
coaxing
is key:
a beckon, tickle
and a
twist.
And as you withdraw,
there she lies -
all scooped out,
fleshy as a cut tongue,
lank and beautiful in vulnerability.
The shell is ripe for crushing now, carved and vacant,
but I've seen many
bathed
post-mortem
of their garlic glisten,
resting hollowed on window ledges.
Opalescent in eggshell blue and lilac -
perfect for filling
with rainwater,
garden weeds,
your little degradations,
your unwavering righteousness.

June

the sun is a bottle top/flipped skyward and dazzling/and
look how small our shadows are in that majesty/our black
clouds/our weighted rucksacks/just tiny tinted
dancefloors/
all bodies look healthier sun-gazed/sun-tan scented and
oil-slicked/youth oozing from the mouth in
ripples of soil/and fertility/like strawberries on the tongue
and pips in the gums so/I'll disguise myself in this mirage
of vitality.

Look how small my shadow is now.

high noon sun/juice dripping chin/small as your
words/small as a penny/small as Old Man Sun could
make me/the thorning tongue you're nurturing won't
notice/not the raising eyebrow/or the peeking buds of
your eyes and

look how small my shadow is now.

I promise it won't encroach on yours/unfurling/
elongated with the dusk/I promise I'll stay small/small like
tan lines/small like baby birds/like bones/like ashes

The Theory of Relationships According to Pythagoras

Point one, and you'd be blind to call this a triangle,
triangular as your limbs all seem;
too many elbows, somehow,
jutted in to left angles,
one too many ribs that make each breath
sound like a butterfly earthquake between chests.
But you embrace like a moulding.
A negative degree angle,
convex,
each cell below the belly button and above the kneecap
part of some complex reaction
fusing into one another,
or
desperate to.

Hearts meet at point two,
Straight lined, so much less about sex these days,
a full-bodied unity.
The points of the hips meet softly now
as breathless kisses,
the sigh of an arm draping a shoulder in triangulation.
These bodies the rise of a steeple, the stretch of a finger,
the swoop of a wing.

But I saw us at point three
obtuse in all angles, repellant;
the touching biceps and minds wandering beyond the
conservatory door.
I'd build a ship in the space between us
and set sail for hope
were it not for the anchor of a tear
against my right-angled shoulder,
and I know these are no seas for mismeasured sails.

I know the triangular warning sign when I see it.

The back pedal got lost, in the angles between hips,
and I'm waiting for point four, an equilateral,
but triangles are only three.

Sponsored by the Office Party

1.

Toast to one last relapse
you say.
My sandpaper tongue is so far down my throat
that I forget to laugh,
forget to ask you
what universe your relapse lives in,
forget to do all else than wonder how your self -
gratification will ripple through my decisions
like it has for the last 5 years.
Tastebuds still wrapped around tonsils,
I can't meet your eye or find the syllable that should be no
and it chimes itself into the clink
of a glass
instead.

2.

In your puffed pink coat,
a tiny dancing candy floss cloud,
I have to stop and admire your bubble-gum innocence.
All rose blossomed cheeks in winter air,
the instability of your confidence,
how every step is just learning
what balance is.

3.

I'm wondering where the lines are
between dressing for my own mind
and finding which dress
is asking for it.
And where the scales balance between confidence and

4.

Slut
you say, disguised as a clogging throat,
do you pay so little attention when
you visit all of your boyfriends

5.

The word
'boyfriend'
is so absent from the pages of my diary
that I begin to wonder
if I'm the right kind of teenager.
The only tongues and grooves I know are the
ridges of my 1980s record player,
and Morrissey's voice sounds like there is something
lodged in his throat.
I like to tell myself that's loneliness.
I think I'm lonely,
but I'm not sure what the balance is between something I
want
and something someone told me I should.

6.

You complimented my body.
The way my clothes cling to the absence of any real
depth
or weight
so that must mean I'm wanted -
right?
That must mean I want this.

7.

I spend my money on bubble-gum and candy floss,
not lip gloss
and none of the other girls meet my eyeline.

8.

The rejection is real
you say, all teeth,
and I'm struggling to find the balance between guilt and
saying what I really want.
To find a single syllable that isn't an inevitable relapse in
my universe,
while
like a candy floss cloud
I struggle to place one foot
in front of the other

Ghosts

There's this thing about train journeys.
Tonight, I'm staring at the Pacman logo/yellow-white
of the 1990s cushioning like it could move.

Train track, *waka waka*,
window crack -
I'm craving that electric repetition.

Not that wind.
How it weeps through the parted mouth
of an open window -
shrieks itself into its own unyielding speed.

Not those passing fields,
because it's blackness outside
so *red* and *bone* and *gut* might not
exist.

waka waka,
train track, spinal clack,
I'm playing that arcade earworm, sing-song
in persistence

because when I let myself listen,
I wonder which pitch of the rails
could make a body disappear.

notes to self on the poem you'll soon write about masturbation

say something about the fact
that you keep
razor blades in the same drawer as you keep
sex toys.

you think about it, constantly.

write something second glancingly
sordid
something penetrative/smooth steel
in places more intimate than your own skin
all finger slits and bodily
fluids
something to make toes curl/knees clench
but maybe not in
that
way.

write something insightful/
rinse out that S&M mouth there's
healing tied to all four bedpost corners and maybe
that drawer
is the pulse of all points *mindful*
and *ecstatic*
and when everything around you feels like it's crumbling
into its own melodrama
and you're suffocating under pillows that belong on
everyone else's beds then go back and
pick from a forbidden menu

of prohibition/prescription/
it's all there for you.
every flavour of feeling.

make yourself
feel
something.

write something about privacy
not *isolation*
not *lonely*
not *desolate/*
those words don't have the iron tang of pornography
or the right shade of red

and don't write too much,
because you're not trying to link together in some
curtained-off back room
any parallel line after line after lines of correlation between
masturbation and self-harm:
don't sound too fucked up.
don't make them feel too fucked up.
but say
I feel numb right now
and
what happens if neither of them
feel like anything
anymore.

Pome

fishbowled through the stomach all bauble and translucent
and churning tail or was that the neck of a snake, my dear,
is that claw or a tooth slitting from the inside

out

pour me empty like a vase when you lose control unzip me
from the sternum I see you peek through a ribcage nibble
at tissue all bile and I'm sorry it hurts I'm sorry I won't
feed you again

(ii)

sad is

memory

and

so much

silence.

Larkin

Your mother
and the way she holds herself like thunderclouds
over a hilltop.
The way each conversation veers itself from the road,
speaking with the ventriloquist inevitability of our pasts.

And I wonder when I began to hate the idea of a child,
or if I hate the idea of a child.

> And your mother again:
> her blood stains the pages of your writing and
> the straight line pink to red of your mouth as you
> repeat the pursed words she taught you and
> it's not her arms anymore
> it's thunderclouds
> and kitchen roll
> and hilltops.

I miss the mountains
so I create my own valleys in the dip of my hips and
wonder if someone will traverse them.
I am too far renounced
from my body to see any beauty
but I'm not sure
anyone
has
noticed.

The earth there is barren, it remains fruitless beyond age,
my mountains are bare and bone
and I wonder if I'll love my child,

and my father speaks through my clamped
tongue and ethanol mouth, and your mother,
and all of our mothers, and we hide in the
shadows of the mountains of our family and our
fuck ups and the layers of our iron weeping
arms and I wonder
how
we
fix
ourselves.

I want to save you but I bled all over the life jackets and
I'm scared
no one
noticed

and that no one will notice

until women and children first and they all continue to
drown.

Cliff

Who sees in this ocean
of false sincerity.

All cliff edge cutting,
bared teeth and tongue,

smile or grimace.
Its softness bears no dimple or scar –

no hand-hold to stop our heads from slipping
below the peer-tide.

And so I tread water.
Brush splayed toes with playful fathers and glowing

mothers, baby's fingers wrapped with diamonds.
Feel seawater sentiment flush out my lungs

and I learn to breathe through biscuit tin photo
albums and Polaroid filtered fireplace memento.

But my lifeline beacon is drowning.
Choking under the crushing wave of belonging,

of proving and pretence.
I couldn't tell you if its gaping mouth

is smile or grimace.
Nor who is happier:

those accepting the deep salt lick of longing,
or those that still pretend they are swimming

If You Were To

You wonder if she'll be disappointed.
She built veins like stained glass cities
and whispers to me when my ribcage rises and falls
with the moon.
That spine is her skyscraper
and I love her for that romanticism.

I can only imagine the jade of her eyes
when the heather begins to bloom between
her shoulder blades,
when Merlot spills from cracked glass elbow creases,
because she speaks to me a lot about dying
but locks the drawer with the knives in.

She whispers to me that the glint in my moonlit eyelashes
looks like a semicolon,
but I know she's sliding an ellipsis down my throat.
And when I close my eyes
the full moon looks like a
                              full
                                        stop.

Albatross

And I took the vices of others.
Wore their personal heartaches as such heavy padding on
each slumping shoulder
that suddenly the deafened spaces between sentences
became razor edged.
Lung submerged.
So I pulled each iris noose from every
'we need to talk' gaze
and draped them around my own muted throat -
too eager to be silenced by the slow choke happiness
of others,
than run riot with the truth of an embittered tongue
The aftermath -
in the end?
It never changed.

Sabatier

How Grandad sharpened knives.
Silhouette against the pantry,
cuticles daring the guard of a whet steel.
White knuckle on that one hand;
the other a flurry of danger and flaking metal
on a stone floor.

My father, after him, took up the fencing arm
of the butcher's steel, rhythmic as aorta,
as a grating bass,
as an almost scream
chimed against the steel pots.

Stomach deep I remember that fleshy grind
in restaurant alleys,
flashing against the dark,
shark teeth from unearthing potholes,
and I apologise for the sharpness of my tongue.
Mastered with inheritance,
chimed against the stone.

Staccato and ridging,
whittled down from the honing steel
of yesterday's conversations.
And you,
the unwilling butcher's cut.
The opened flesh to test my hardness.

You Say Siren

I wait for you to list emeralds and tryptics,
the fleshy roundness of stomachs and lips.
Bouncing curls that bob
up
and down
with the waves.
This song a knife hilt pounding under the breastbone.

I wait for your breathlessness, a rebirthing,
your umbilical undoing
and entire giving.

Later I'll show you the carcass.
That hollowed out jawline, licked out to bone.
I'll paint you an oil canvas in cadmium and rust,
show you skinny jeans and stacks of teeth on bookcases

and next time someone tells you beware a woman,
you'll glance
and set your sail.

My Body; The Forest

Pine damp scented, kneeling
willow, bending and silver
and peeling birch.
These rootless trees,
my feet; swallows upturned and
homeless in too many half-made homes.
Tiny wanderers, unsettle
with my butterfly ribcage.
Bone tickled anxious, buzz saw echoed
through cottontail fingers,
through hedgehog tongue:
furtive,
prickly in truth.
Watch me curl,
armoured,
hiding under all those ivy I Love Yous.
All that wilderness that back garden pickets
never quite allowed.

A What If

Each second loops in mental revisitation.
Flinching hands over glass ledges,
and words we'll claim were never spoken,
through unsolicited blushes and table hidden touch.
Adrenaline anticipation, and the suffocation of knowing
that across a dimension,
if we could sidle through the gaps between each universe -
cradled in blankets of predetermined, soul-told stardust -
each park-lit walk, each skittish giggle, every half-brushed
inch of skin
may be
could be
life existent beyond the forbidden.

And maybe that's why,
in pastiche daydream memory,
as my mouth finds mimicry of our suppression-led grin,
I don't recall the moment our eyes met.
Those mood-stone constellations stay firmly planted on
hesitant ground:
neither of us so far taken with irresponsibility
to let those galaxies ruinously collide.

In this universe
a 'what if'
will remain enough.

8

Last night I watched the sun die.
Leak outside the outlines
slough yellow
sanguine draining
woeful crimson burning.
Some of us
placed tissue paper squares across the sky,
tried to blot out our inevitable
our gaping omen
our clumsy colouring,
but Old Grandfather sun -
he bled through the clouds in blots and
pulse and seep.
Dripped and soaked and streaked in amber
and some of us were scared
and some of us were angry
but I think the sun was sad
and
I just wanted to say I'm sorry for every second of
magnificent you that I ever missed.
I fold these 8.2 minutes
close your eyes
open your hands
and place them in the safe creases of your palms.

So Let's Call This Thing a House

Shall I describe it to you?

See, I have to explain
that she needs a little care,
so if I tell you about the brickwork -
its crumble and shy from the touch -
then hear the apologies to her bloodrust stone
for building on such uneven grounding.
Venetian, she sinks in sighs,
foundations pinned to the spaces in the earth
where someone surely was before,
but never stayed.

I should tell you now how she wraps her shallow frame
in a throw of ivy green,
each tendril clinging to the undersides of grazes
and the backs of knees,
to the glint of a tooth and the stitch of budding mouths:
let's call her a wild silence.
Let's call this thing a house.

So, if I tell you about the hole in the ground floor window,
then see her button nose wearing away at the glass
as it presses towards the moon.
She's carved herself skylights to see the constellations
breathe in and out of her in a pulse,
moulding in to splits and creases to manipulate her own
shadow.

I've seen stars
streak her drainpipe thighs
when the world has shut its eyes.
When the earth has looked away just long enough to
siphon off the sun -
though I should say
how her emptiness clots the rain in feathers and down:
let's call her a matted sadness,
pull out bones from the debris.

And if I tell you again
let's call this thing a house
then paint the door canary yellow and throw it open.
Build me a corridor of birds to drown in,
make a room for the butterflies:
let's call this a wild undoing

My love,
run those fingers across her stretch marks and sigh,
and we'll call this thing a home.

(iii)

~~sad~~ hope is

hearts

preserved

it's

memory
it's

particular shade of

sunshine

it's

the sound you get
when you place the right shell to your ear
and
hear
~~silence~~
everything.

Duo

So here you arrived,
breathy with cat-purr longing
and a ripening moan -
those tiny deaths
that make lips tremble in syncopation
with wind-chime knees.

And did you strike your tuning fork against my thigh
to perfect that open sesame pitch at the base of your
throat?
Or did we always sing from the same half-sheet of a
symphony?

And did you know karaoke means empty orchestra in
Japanese?

Like a string section with no violin,
like an acapella troupe with no harmonies,
like a missing baton,
like I'll be the indie singer in your band,
like I'll be anything for you
when you exhale that way.

Affirmations - #1

Throw away the mirrors, love.
Discard the bubbling and bruise.

Remember how each flower knows herself
bulbous and full
as gentle earth rolls her into vibrancy.

Remember the edges of glass -
the empty transparency.
Remind yourself that invisibility is not a gift,
nor a fortune;
that sharpness cannot kiss and does not caress.
That glass will not grow.

So plant yourself in the ground, love.
Throw away the mirrors.
Grow fruits in the reflections of strangers' smiles.
Paint your fences yellow.
Hang ivy from the walls.

Solstice

The longest period of sunshine.

The most hours of pupil dilated daylight.

She spent today cocooned between bird nest and haystack. Comforted in the arms of gentle tree-strung fairy dusting and even gentler company. Cradled between culture and care.

And she thought about the many lives lived on this day. How she welcomed elongated shadows in roller skate suburbia, how her tastebuds melted in BBQ relish, how she used to tribal thump to a Druid drumbeat amongst strange friends and friendlier strangers.

But, to unfurl a tongue in honesty (like those stone shadows erecting themselves in honour of daybreak and time), she gave no gratitude to the pleasures of today. In no way to say she scorned them. Ignored them. She heard the sunset patter of nested beaks. She felt the rushes of passion. She saw the layered beauty of dusk amongst trees, of smiling infant faces, of blossoming affections. She appreciated all through a layer of numbness. An age yellowed haze. A watching of her own self, and every self, on reclaimed film reels against a darkened wall.

The longest period of sunshine, and she could only wish for eternal twilight. An endless dusk.

I could make this a tale of how every tree became barbed wire and bladed branch, every road stretch yearning jaws and shaking hands holding Alice's 'Eat Me' pills, but this isn't that kind of poem.

Because she lived.

Through the longest period of sunshine. The most hours of pupil dilated daylight. She kept her eyes open against every weight that whispered the glory of closure.

We all did.

We carried on, to discover the hope warmed splendour - in whichever muted palette we perceive it - that our next sunrise promises.

Whitby

Tonight, I'll press my nose
to the stomach of the moon.
Feel its soft lacking against my forehead,
and place the cold innards of teaspoons
against my eyelids,
wondering what to do
with all of this extra gravity.

Tomorrow we will wake:
waxing, fuller bellied,
swollen in idolatry.
So full of beautiful weight, little moon.
So full of light.

ACKNOWLEDGEMENTS

Huge thanks and gratitude to all of the following, who have been instrumental in the creation of the dew point:

Stuart Bartholomew and Verve Poetry Press for all the time, effort and encouragement in bringing this work to life.

The fabulous Nick Degg, Jemima Hughes and John MacLeod for being my manuscript guinea pigs.

Poetry for the People and The Lichfield Poets for pushing me to take my baby steps into the poetic world. This wouldn't exist without you.

My wonderful family, for their constant support. To my parents, for their exceptional music taste that shaped my writing from an early age. To my sister, for being a daily inspiration in her creativity and talent.

All the friends that have taken the time to support, read, and listen to these pieces over the last few years. I've never been able to thank you enough to your faces.

Staffordshire County Council and Staffordshire Libraries for taking a chance on a young woman that wanted to be the first female Poet Laureate of the county.

Chris Wilson and the WordCraft Spoken Word community for their unending support and love. You fill up my heart every single month.

All the poetry communities I've had the fortune to encounter, who have been so welcoming and kind. It's been an absolute joy to meet, perform, and develop relationships with such talented and wonderful humans. Special shout outs to the folks in Worcester and Stoke-on-Trent, who have taken me so gently under their wings.

Phillip Knight for being my poetry instigator, confidence booster and constant mentor. Your faith in this work has been unfaltering, and your encouragement unparalleled.

ABOUT VERVE POETRY PRESS

Verve Poetry Press is a quite new and already award-winning press that focused initially on meeting a local need in Birmingham - a need for the vibrant poetry scene here in Brum to find a way to present itself to the poetry world via publication. Co-founded by Stuart Bartholomew and Amerah Saleh, it now publishes poets from all corners of the UK - poets that speak to the city's varied and energetic qualities and will contribute to its many poetic stories.

Added to this is a colourful pamphlet series, many featuring poets who have performed at our sister festival - and a poetry show series which captures the magic of longer poetry performance pieces by festival alumni such as Polarbear, Matt Abbott and Genevieve Carver.

The press has been voted Most Innovative Publisher at the Saboteur Awards, and has won the Publisher's Award for Poetry Pamphlets at the Michael Marks Awards.

Like the festival, we strive to think about poetry in inclusive ways and embrace the multiplicity of approaches towards this glorious art.

www.vervepoetrypress.com
@VervePoetryPres
mail@vervepoetrypress.com